21 DAYS TO BETTER BOUNDARIES

A GUIDE TO SETTING BOUNDARIES WITH KINDNESS + COMPASSION

ANN WEISER CORNELL, PH.D.

CALLUNA PRESS | BERKELEY, CALIFORNIA

CALLUNA PRESS
2342 Shattuck Ave #413, Berkeley CA 94704
510.225.0690

Design and layout: Maggie Hurley
Content Editor: Shannon Crossman

ISBN: 978-0-9721058-8-0
eISBN: 978-0-9721058-9-7

For Barbara McGavin, creative partner, without whom none of this would be possible.

CONTENTS

Introduction

It was a summer night and I was 17, out on a first date with a guy I didn't know very well. We were sitting on the grass, drinking wine... and then he put his hand on my thigh, under my skirt. My heart started pounding, but not with passion. This was going too fast and I was scared. But I didn't know I had a right to express my doubts. I didn't have a voice.

Luckily, someone walked by us and the mood changed, and I took the opportunity to head for a safer environment. But there were other evenings, other dates, and many other instances of feeling confused and unsure what I felt, what I wanted, and whether I had a right to my own feelings and wants.

In the years since then I've learned how to know what I feel, and how to value what I need. I've learned that, in relationships, I have a right to my own voice. I've learned how to include the other person in a back-and-forth where I don't get swamped but I also don't dominate them. These lessons were not easy ones, and I've often wished I had more great models of people setting healthy boundaries.

My students and clients also struggle with setting healthy boundaries, and a few years ago I created a course that would not only be about healthy boundaries, but would actually be 21 practices, a new one every day, to make healthy boundaries a reality. People found that course so life-changing that I decided to turn it into this book. In creating and teaching that course, I realized having healthy boundaries brings together so much of what is important about emotional healing and personal growth.

Healthy Boundaries are about:

- your worth as a person

- your right to your own voice

- your own needs and values

- your mutual connections with other people

- and so much more

A healthy boundary is flexible, not rigid, and is able to honor various factors such as: What are my values and needs? What kind of relationship is this? How do we need to connect in the future?

What do I mean by boundary?

A boundary might be the line between your needs and another person's needs, your time and another person's time, your feelings and another person's feelings. It could also be within yourself, between your work life and your life-life!

If healthy boundaries are challenging, it's usually because of our history. How healthy were the boundaries in your family? What are the expectations you grew up with? Did you have encouragement to draw a boundary and say, "Stop, that's far enough" — and have it respected?

In this book, you'll learn a series of practices to become aware of the challenges you experience around boundaries. You'll also get to practice creating new habits of awareness and communication that work better for you than what you've been doing.

The practices are designed to be done daily. Each day you work with a new practice. I'll give you a suggested practice for the day, and I recommend you put it into practice for the next 24 hours. And you can always come back to specific sections to practice more.

Maybe you can think right now at what time of day you'll have 10-15 minutes every day to really concentrate on the material. All I ask of you is 10-15 minutes once a day, as close to the same time each day as possible. And then for the next 24 hours, keep the practice in mind, try it out when appropriate and then you'll be ready for the next one.

Want some additional support? Sign up for access to **free videos, audio exercises, and more resources** for setting better boundaries here: https://focusingresources.com/hbfree

Otherwise, let's get started!

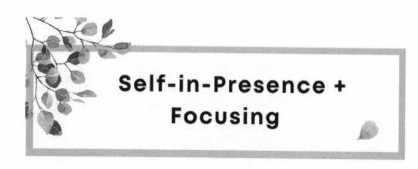

Self-in-Presence + Focusing

T here are two key terms you will need to get the most out of this book: *Self-in-Presence* and *Focusing*.

Self-in-Presence is our word for your ability to bring a spacious, healing presence to your stressful emotional states. You *have* feelings, but you *are not* your feelings. You can be with how you feel, rather than being caught up in or carried away by how you feel. This is a key concept (a key skill) and we'll be developing it throughout this book.

Focusing is a process of self-awareness that allows you to explore and process your emotional reactions to life situations. Your blocks and triggers can begin to release. This book includes easy and supportive Focusing exercises specifically for releasing issues around setting boundaries. At the end of the book we will tell you how to learn more about Focusing if you want to go further.

DAY 1

The Most Important Boundary to Set First

The most important boundary to set first is your own inner boundary between being identified with your emotional states and being Self-in-Presence.

Today's practice is Creating Relationship with Your Emotional States.

This is the most important boundary to set first because if you're merged with or identified with your emotional states, and they take you over, you may find yourself doing or saying things you later regret. Or the opposite, being paralyzed with inaction and later regretting that. Furthermore, an emotional state you're identified with cannot be explored very effectively.

And in the next 21 days we are going to be doing a lot of emotional exploring!

So what I invite you to practice today, and to make a habit of as you work through this book, is to say the words *"something in me"* when you're talking about your emotional states relating to boundaries.

In other words, *"I'm worried about rejection"* would become *"something in me is worried about rejection."*

"I feel scared when I think about facing another person's anger" would become *"something in me feels scared when I think about facing another person's anger."*

See how that works? Now you try it.

Let's pause for a moment for you to **sense how you're feeling as you start this 21-day practice.**

Now try these steps:

ONE: Make a three-word sentence stating a challenging or uncomfortable feeling you have about setting boundaries, like "I am scared" or "I feel apprehensive."

(This works best with challenging feelings. If you feel eager or excited, you don't need to dis-identify from those.)

If you don't feel anything right now that's challenging or hard, you might remember another time recently when you felt upset or irritated or worried. Just to use for the practice.

TWO: Change your sentence by adding "something in me"- as in "something in me feels scared" or "something in me feels apprehensive."

For example: "I am scared." → "Something in me is scared."

Or: "I feel worried." → "Something in me feels worried."

See how that works? Easy!

THREE: Add the words, "And I am saying hello to that something."

Like this: "Something in me is scared. And I am saying hello to that something."

Notice what difference that makes. Most people find they can be with the feeling more comfortably, ready to get curious about it and get to know it better.

What's important about the "something in me" language is that you're creating a relationship with your emotional states. Creating that relationship is really important because:

- You're not pushing away or dismissing how you feel

- You're not getting taken over by how you feel

- You'll be able to explore the feelings with curiosity

You have a perspective in which it becomes possible for new behaviors to emerge

By the way, there's another important reason I wanted to start the book with this practice. That has to do with getting overwhelmed.

Setting healthy boundaries is a huge issue for many of us. It can bring up a lot of stuff about our own identity, our needs, our families, and perhaps our trauma history as well. Anyone could potentially get overwhelmed by all of that.

But when you're overwhelmed, you can't process very well. You can't think clearly or react appropriately to the present.

Overwhelm can be an important message from your inner being. Let's respect it, and give compassion and care to the overwhelmed "something" in you. It may well be a signal to go more slowly.

The best way to safely do inner work and emotional exploring is to respect the signals that something is too much right now. And take your time.

Today's practice: As you go through your daily life, I recommend you be aware of how you're feeling. If it's not easy to know how you're feeling in the moment, you might give yourself "pause breaks" to take a few minutes to check in with yourself. (Would once an hour work for you?)

Then, when you know how you're feeling, and if it's a challenging feeling like "upset" rather than "joyous," practice saying *"something in me feels _____"* and *"I am saying hello to that."* And feeling what difference that makes.

Remember: "Something in me feels ____ and I am saying hello to that."

First Aid for Overwhelm

Any time you feel overwhelmed as you work with boundaries, here's what you can do:

- Pause and get grounded, i.e. breathe and feel your contact with the ground.

- Say the words, "Something in me is feeling overwhelmed," and notice what happens.

- If the overwhelm is accompanied by a body sensation, let a gentle hand go there to the place where you feel that.

- Say "Hello" to the "something in you" feeling overwhelmed.

- Listen to what it needs from you right now... perhaps a break? Some time to recover?

DAY 2

Your Right to Honor Your Own Needs

Honoring your needs doesn't mean
always going for them. It does mean
always respecting them.

Your Day Two practice is Knowing that You Have a Right to Honor Your Own Needs.

The issue of setting healthy boundaries often has to do with honoring our own needs. And let's make a clear distinction that honoring your needs is not the same as asserting them. I can honor my needs and still decide not to assert them. Does that make sense?

It can be extremely helpful to make a two-step separation between the internal feeling and the outer action.

Number one: I can know what I feel.

Number two: I can decide what to do about it, including nothing.

In my earlier life, this was a very mixed up and confusing distinction. Looking back, I realize I didn't have much of a private inner world. If I thought my feelings wouldn't be welcomed by others, it was hard for me to know what my feelings even were.

Over time and with a lot of inner practice, I've become able to know how I feel without having to show it, and to know how I feel even in settings where I wouldn't want to show it, where it wouldn't be safe... or polite.

So what I'm saying is that you have a right to honor your own needs, and by that I mean:

- To know what they are.

- To take them into account.

- To know that your own needs are legitimate, they're valid, they're just as worthwhile as anyone else's needs.

- To get in touch with what you need is already a kind of honoring.

It's a further honoring to acknowledge that your needs are valid.

Let me take a moment to define what I mean by "needs."

Here I'd like to follow the teaching of Marshall Rosenberg that needs are universal to all humans. And that needs are different from strategies to meet those needs. I don't *need* you to do the dishes. I might *like* you to do the dishes. My *need* would be for cooperation, mutuality, or support… that kind of thing.

I find it really helps to make that distinction between needs and strategies because it helps me get unhooked from a particular thing I want the other person to do, or a particular thing they want me to do. I remember needs are universal, so of course all needs can be honored. (For more about the teaching of Marshall Rosenberg, also known as Nonviolent Communication, check out https://www.cnvc.org/)

You have a right to honor your own needs AND you have a right to honor your own feelings. Both are important and worth being in touch with. And both are separate from what we decide to do or speak up about.

Let's give this a try right now, OK?

I know for many people — because they've told me — it can be hard to know what they feel and need in the heat of the moment. So let's practice by taking something you felt in the past. (I know you'd like to know what you feel and need in the moment but we can work up to that. This is the place to start.)

Pause and think of a time fairly recently (in the past week would be ideal, but if something from longer ago comes that's OK) when you were confused or sort of numb in an interaction with another person. Maybe you were going on autopilot, and you realize now you weren't in touch with your feelings and needs, or not completely.

Take a moment here to find that experience for yourself before you continue.

Once you're aware of that situation (but you're no longer actually in it), try these steps:

ONE: Imagine you're sitting next to yourself as a listener.

Sit by that younger version of you, even if only one week younger! Be the listener to that person. Say to this "younger you" that you'd like to help them get in touch with what they need.

TWO: Wait. Be patient.

Real feelings and needs can take time to emerge. (Often we don't know what we need because no one, including us, has had this kind of patience!)

Imagine you could stop time and the person you were last week (or whenever) now has all the time in the world, all the time they need to find out what they really *feel* in that situation. And then also what they really *need*.

THREE: When the feelings and needs emerge, simply hear them and honor them.

If there's a challenging feeling like frustrated or sad or upset then there's probably also an unmet need. Take your time to just listen.

Remember that feelings are often unclear at first. They need time. And giving them time, as you're doing now, is a very respectful thing to do. If honoring your feelings and needs is new for you, really take time to sense how it feels to do this.

You might also notice whether you feel you have a right to have your own needs, that your needs are worthwhile. We're not talking about what you tell others about what you need. We're separating that out for now. This is about your right to have your own needs and to know within yourself what they are.

If you can feel there's a part of you that isn't sure you have that right, let's turn toward that part for a little while. Just let it know you hear it. Sense how it feels, and give it some company. Good. There's no need to do anything else. No need to tell it anything. Just be a listener.

That's the huge practice today. You can be your own inner listener. And listening involves getting how it is. It doesn't involve trying to change it. Change emerges from allowing space for how it is.

If you've found a part of you that isn't sure you have a right to honor your own needs, I'm pretty sure it's a younger part of you, I mean quite a bit younger. And I'm pretty sure it would appreciate you coming back to it today, several times.

Enjoy! This work can be amazingly transformational, one step at a time.

Remember: You have a right to have your own feelings and needs, and to know what they are.

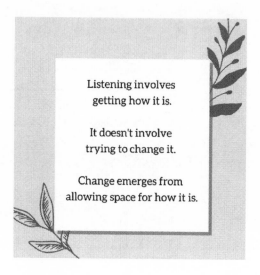

Listening involves
getting how it is.

It doesn't involve
trying to change it.

Change emerges from
allowing space for how it is.

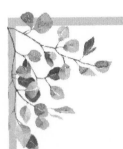

DAY 3

Setting Boundaries without Anger, Blaming, Excuses, or Apologies

You don't need to get angry or blame others in order to set boundaries, and you also don't need to apologize or make excuses.

T oday, let's talk about the Superpower of Setting Boundaries without Anger, Blaming, Excuses, or Apologies.

Wouldn't it be amazing to be able to do that? Wouldn't it be amazing to draw your line and say, "I'm afraid not," or "No, that won't work for me," and not feel the internal pressure to:

- get angry;

- blame the other person for asking;

- make excuses; and

- apologize.

When I say "apologize," I'm not talking about something short like "I'm sorry" or "No, that won't work for me, I'm sorry." (It doesn't hurt to be nice!)

I'm talking about the kind of apology that goes on and on and basically communicates that *I'm not sure I have the right to say this.*

All four of the things we're talking about today — getting angry, blaming, making excuses, and profuse apologies — they all spring from not feeling you have the right to say "No, this is my boundary." Check if one of these styles of boundary-setting sounds familiar:

Anger: "I hate being put in this position!"

Blaming: "If you'd planned better you wouldn't need to be asking me for this."

Excuses: "I can't do it because my cat is sick, and I've been way over my head this week, and my parents are coming this weekend, and anyway I'm just too tired."

Apologies: "I'm so so sorry, it's terrible that I can't help you with this, I really wish I could..."

Take a moment to feel the difference between any of the above and something simple and direct like: "No, I'm afraid that won't work for me."

Notice... it's not just the words, there's also an inner place where the words come from, a kind of calm confidence that it's OK to say No. You have a right to your boundary.

Yesterday, you practiced having the right to honor your own needs, even if you don't do anything to express them to others. Today, we're talking about having the right to set your boundary with another person.

Now, I know that the whole thing about setting boundaries is complex. In later sections we're going to get into issues such as fear of the other person's response, our own sense of guilt or responsibility, being able to separate our feelings from the other person's feelings, and lots more. There are many factors.

So today, just to get started, I invite you to imagine a simple situation.

Someone you don't know asks you for something. You're in public in the daytime, you're not in danger, and it doesn't meet your needs to say *yes*, so you say *no*. Simple.

It should be simple! But many of us aren't sure we even have the right to say *no* in a simple situation like that. So it's the perfect "laboratory" to practice the No Anger, No Blame, No Excuses, No Apologies method of setting your boundary.

So put yourself in that imaginary situation. What might a stranger ask you for? Where I live, it's often money. "Can you spare some change?" You might want to say *yes* to someone like that. But for our practice today, let's say you want to say *no*.

If being asked for money in the street is not simple for you, take a moment to imagine a more simple situation that is not fraught with a lot of extra factors. A friend asks you to watch her dog or a co-worker asks you to stay late... I don't know what it would be for you, but we're looking for a situation that should be simple. Of course even supposedly simple situations often aren't — and that's the point of today's practice.

So the person asks you what they ask you and now let's freeze time. How do you feel? Put upon? Angry? Resentful? "How dare they"? Or guilty? Apologetic?

Take some time to sense.

If you feel anything other than a simple confidence that it's OK to say *no*... then let's use the "something in me" language we already learned in order to turn toward that feeling.

Like "something in me feels angry at being asked."

"I'm saying hello to that."

"I'm asking it, What is it about being asked this, that gets it so angry?"

And listen...

Whatever the feeling is, angry, resentful, put upon, guilty... you're just going to listen.

What you might discover, that I think is very interesting, is something like: this gets me angry or resentful or put upon or guilty because I don't like setting boundaries!

So now, in this very simple imaginary situation, let yourself say a very simple *no*. Like, "No, I'm afraid that won't work for me." Or just, "No, sorry." And smile. Just practice that a few times, finding the way of saying it that sounds natural for you.

Remember, in a real situation there are always extra complications! So all you're doing today is practicing what it feels like to say *no* without anger, blame, excuses, or apologies in an ideally simple situation. Just so you know it is possible sometimes.

Change comes in steps, and this is a step.

So: "No, I'm afraid that won't work for me." Or just, "No, sorry." And smile.

And then notice how that feels.

If it feels awkward and strange, that's very understandable!

The practice for today is to mentally rehearse a simple way of saying *no* without anger, blame, excuses or apologies. You can imagine a simple situation as in this chapter. Or you can use the situations you encounter today. But no need to actually say this out loud to anyone! The mental rehearsal is the practice for today.

Remember: No Anger, No Blame, No Excuses, No Apologies. And for today, just mental practice.

If you find an emotional part of you that needs attention

As you imagine responding to requests with a calm and simple *no*, you may discover a part of you that feels anger at the request, or resentful, or put upon, or apologetic. Here is a way to give some attention to a part like that.

1. Choose a time during your day when you won't be interrupted for about 15 minutes.

2. Settle in and feel your breathing and your body grounding.

3. Imagine a person making a request that you want to say no to. You can use the imaginary simple situation from the chapter, or something else. Notice how you react emotionally to the request.

4. Use the language of "Something in me feels…" to acknowledge and turn toward the emotional part of you.

5. Be a listener to that part of you. Be curious what's going on for IT from its point of view. It might show you images or memories rather than speaking in words. Whatever it shows you or lets you know, just listen. This is not a time for you to tell it anything. "I hear you, and I'm open to more…"

6. If you feel any kind of shift in your body, like a deeper breath or a sense of release, take some time to enjoy that before stopping.

You might also sense if this is something that wants you to return to it for more listening. You can let it know you're willing to do that.

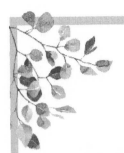

DAY 4

Being Aware, in the Moment, That There's a Boundaries Issue

Is this a boundaries issue?
Here are the clues...

Y esterday, you practiced with an artificially simple situation, so you could feel what it's like to say *no* calmly, with confidence. So you could experiment with knowing you have the right to say *no*... and therefore there's no need to apologize or make excuses or get angry or feel resentful.

And we said that in real situations there are often complications. Well, one of those complications is that **it can be unclear, in the moment, that a situation involves/includes a boundaries issue.**

Why? Well, one reason is that there are a lot of interactions where the other person doesn't make a simple, direct request. With no simple direct request, we're in an odd position. It can be confusing. I'm not sure if the other person asked me for something or not. They certainly didn't ask directly, but did they ask indirectly? Only my uneasy feeling gives me a clue that something is going on!

I know this kind of situation really well. In my family of origin people rarely made direct requests. There was more of a feeling, like an underlying unquestioned assumption, that of course we were going to meet the other person's needs when they were revealed to us in indirect ways. My mother especially was a master of the Hint! Questions were used as indirect orders. "Have you done your homework yet?" was a relatively simple one. There were others that were much more indirect.

Notice how hard it is to respond cleanly to "Have you done your homework yet?" It's a Yes-No question, but only *yes* is an acceptable answer. Saying *no* gets you in trouble. The question itself backs you up against the wall. If you'd decided to do your homework later, there's no easy way to say that.

This was another place where Marshall Rosenberg's Non-Violent Communication method was a lifesaver for me. I learned it was possible to make simple requests and allow the other person the freedom to say *yes* or *no*. (If the other person doesn't have the freedom to say *no*, Marshall calls that a "demand," not a "request.")

You can also do the same thing in reverse. You can guess at the request the other person is making, even if they say something very indirect, like, "It's such a hot day." Is that a request for a glass of lemonade? Or for me to turn on the fan? Or is it just a simple statement?

You know, it's because the whole area of making requests and possibly being rejected is so fraught that people end up making these indirect statements. There are also cultures where it's impolite to ask directly. But we can at least be aware that such a thing may be happening... and as usual, awareness goes a long way toward making us free.

Do you encounter this kind of situation, where you're not sure if the other person is making a request? Do you ever find yourself in interactions where you feel an unspoken pressure to do something for the other person, but that's never put into words or made explicit so you'd have the power to clarify it and say *yes* or *no*?

For example, you might be talking to your cousin about her son who lives in your city. Let's say your cousin says, "I wish I could just know on a regular basis that he was OK."

Do you feel an inner urge to offer to check up on your cousin's son every week and let her know how he is doing? Did your cousin make that request? Or was she simply expressing a wish with no pressure on you?

It can be really hard to tell! And if it's hard to tell what the request is, it's also hard to identify what you want, and to say a clear *yes* or *no*.

In that scenario, imagine saying to the cousin something like, "I'm not clear whether you're asking me something or not... are you?" Yes, you have a right to clarify whether you're receiving a request, and then decide how you want to respond.

If this rings a bell, take a moment right now to remember an instance where you were in a similar kind of unclear situation.

What request did you feel like the other person was making, in an indirect way? If they were making a request directly, what would that request have been? Take some time to put that into words.

Now ask yourself, *How would that situation have changed for me if I had gotten a direct request rather than an indirect one? Would it have been easier to know where I stood? Would it have been easier to respond?*

Imagine you could have asked the person something like, "Do you have a request for me?" Or said something like, "I'm not clear whether you're asking me something or not... are you?"

And notice if the situation shifts for you when you have that kind of clarity.

Good!

So your practice for today is... As you go through the interactions of your life, face-to-face conversations, phone calls, emails... Ask yourself, "Is there a request here? Do I know what it is?"

That's the practice. To listen for requests. Because unless we can clarify what the request is, we don't have much chance to separate what the other person is asking from how we'd like to respond.

Until we can clarify what the request is, we don't even know if it's a boundary issue. Once we know, we can practice our growing Superpower of being able to honor and say what we need.

Remember: "Is there a request here? Do I know what it is?"

DAY 5

Saying No Without Fear of Being Abandoned and Alone

The part of you that's afraid you'll be cast out if you set boundaries needs gentle attention.

Today we're going to look at one of the reasons why setting boundaries in relationships can be so challenging.

It's the fear that if you don't give the other person what they're asking for, the relationship will end and you'll be abandoned and alone.

We can understand that fear. It's scary to lose a relationship. You can have compassion for the part of you that would do anything to hang onto this person. But it's a *part* of you, not *all* of you.

And like so many of the emotional issues that come up as you work with boundaries, this ties back to your earlier life — to a time when you really were dependent on other people for your survival — your parents or other caregivers.

It can be very scary to be a child. A parent held up by an accident, coming home hours later than expected = a terrified child, staring into the stark horror of being left alone, uncared for and unfed, forever.

That much could happen by mistake. But for many of us, the threat of losing our parents' love and care was deliberately held over us. "Be good or I'll sell you to the ragman." Sounds like a joke, but children are quite literal. To a sensitive child, that's no joke.

The result, when you grow to adulthood, can be a kind of inner clutching to a relationship that may not be serving your needs in its present form, but it's easy to think it's better than no relationship at all.

I remember a moment when I was 18. I had spent the summer with my boyfriend in a city far from home, and we were packing to return to college. The relationship had many problems and we'd just had one of our horrible fights. Then he left for a while. I was by myself. And I thought, "I could break up with him. I could go back to college as my own person, independent and free." There was a delightful feeling of strength and wholeness. And then the backlash came. I found myself looking into my own core and finding nothing there but darkness. No, I couldn't break up with him. I simply couldn't bear to be alone.

I often wonder what might have happened if I'd had Focusing back then, or a kind friend who could have listened to my feelings. Perhaps the darkness I felt at the core of me could have been healed. Perhaps I could have understood that darkness as coming from my unresolved childhood fears... and I could have given a healing quality of compassion to that Younger Me. But I didn't have those resources.

An adult relationship wants to be a relationship where both people are of equal value. It's not OK if one person wins all the time. There is respect, there is give and take, there is listening. We include our differences rather than trying to pretend we don't have any.

What it means to be a full partner in a relationship is that you're in touch with what you feel and what you need, and you hold your needs along with your awareness of the other person's needs. And that's true whether this is a romantic relationship, a marriage, a friendship, or a family.

But what if it doesn't feel that way? What if you *do* have fear that trying to be an equal partner in this relationship will lead to disaster?

Let's separate out two sides to that question. One is your own history, the hurt child inside you that you'd be bringing to any relationship until the wound is healed. Then there's the other person, the one you're in a relationship with now, and how they react to you stating your needs.

We're going to work in a later section with how to relate to other people's feelings. This one, today, is for working with your own. And never doubt that changing your own inner relationship can change your outer relationships as well. Because the outer is a mirror of the inner.

If you have a fear that's stopping you from setting the boundaries you need to have a healthy life, there are a few things to understand:

- This fear springs from an earlier time in your life when you had fewer resources.

- The part of you that has the fear is younger than your adult self.

- Hiding what you feel and need out of fear doesn't lead to a healthy relationship. On the contrary.

Let's acknowledge that the process of healing the fear of being abandoned and alone may take some time. And we can start today.

Here's how to give company to the Younger You who might be carrying an old fear of abandonment.

Let's start by having you cultivate your own resources so you can be Self-in-Presence. Remember that's the larger You that can be with anything that comes.

Take your time to sense your body in contact with what supports you. And rest into that support. Perhaps you could say the words, "I am the space where all my feelings can be as they are."

Now bring awareness into the inner area of your body: your throat, your chest, your stomach area.

Say (out loud or inwardly): "Perhaps there's something in me that's afraid that if I assert my boundaries, I'll be alone."

Now just wait. The "something" that's afraid may come into your awareness slowly. It may be a body feeling, an image, or even just a sense that something is there but hiding.

When the "something" comes, treat it gently. This is a "younger you." Sense how it would like to be treated by you.

There is a healing presence in simply being there with this "younger you" who is afraid. There's no need to try to change its feelings. In fact, *trying* to change will hold back change. Just be there for at least a few minutes. Very good.

Let's complete this process by having you thank and appreciate your body. Knowing that you will be able to return when you want, to your relationship with the "younger you."

Remember — and this is very important — YOU are not the same as the "younger you" who is afraid. And the "younger you" who is afraid right now needs to feel that you're there with them. That's a process that changes things. The hurt, scared child starts to heal. Like all healing, this is a beautiful and natural process. You just need to be there, to be present, for it to happen.

Your practice today is to visit that younger part of you that you found in today's exercise. Perhaps a few times.

You can repeat the whole exercise or you can just bring awareness to your body and say Hello to that "younger you."

Remember to gather your resources so you know YOU are larger than the scared part of you.

Another practice for today is to do something for yourself to cultivate your inner resources. That might be: taking a walk in nature, looking at something beautiful, meditating, yoga, napping...

Feel free to stop any time. Even short periods of this kind of inner company are valuable. If it ever feels like too much, that's a trustworthy signal. You can stop and come back later. Do you remember the "First Aid for Overwhelm" I gave you on the very first day? It's still there if you need it, just after Day One.

Remember: Visit the "younger you" who is afraid of getting abandoned and just say, "I am with you now."

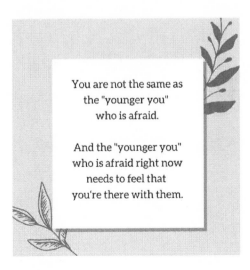

You are not the same as
the "younger you"
who is afraid.

And the "younger you"
who is afraid right now
needs to feel that
you're there with them.

DAY 6

Saying Yes

Healthy boundaries are really about saying Yes.

Healthy boundaries aren't just about saying *no*. They're also about saying *yes*...

Yes with an open heart, *yes* to what matters to you, *yes* to contributing and giving when doing so nurtures you and your relationships.

You've been doing some deep exploring in the first five days of this journey. Today I'd like to lighten things up a bit. Healthy boundaries are also about saying *yes*... wholeheartedly. If you have a right to say *no*, you can also say a real *yes*.

Many of us grew up without really being given the right to say *no*. Often a *yes* was forced out of us. But that's not a real *yes*, is it? Our power to say *yes* is based on our power to say *no* sometimes!

Imagine that you're at home in your house or apartment or wherever it is you live. Imagine there's a very good friend, someone you'd love to see, and you've invited your friend to come over. (If you don't have a friend like that in your life right now, you can create an imaginary friend, perhaps someone from a book or movie you enjoy.)

So you're at home and your friend is coming over. You hear they've arrived. You go to the door and open it, and there's your friend. Hello!

Now let's freeze time so you can pause and sense what's going on for you at this moment.

This is the door to your home. There's a boundary around your home and the door is where you let people in. Take some time to notice how it feels to have the power to willingly invite this person in, across your threshold.

You don't have to let them in! You could change your mind. You could say, "I'm sorry, I know I invited you over but there's been a crisis and I need you to come back later." If you *had* to let them in, if you had no choice, then your *yes* wouldn't have much value, would it? You can say a wholehearted "Yes!" because you also had the right and the power to say *no*.

After you feel your right to let this person in or not, go ahead and allow them in. Notice what it feels like to willingly allow someone in through your door. They didn't break down your door. You could have said *no*. In fact, you said *yes*.

> "Knock knock"
> "Who's there?"

It sounds like the beginning of a joke. But it's also a way to practice your right to set a boundary around who comes into your space and who doesn't.

Now imagine someone you really don't like comes to your door.

> "Knock knock"
> "Who's there?"
> "Dracula."
> "No... I'm not at home for you."

A boundary, your boundary, is a place where you have the right to say *yes* or *no*. "Yes, you may cross, you may enter." Or "No, you may not cross, you may not enter."

Pause a moment and let yourself feel what it's like to have that power. The power to open the door and invite your friend in, or the power to keep it closed and send out the message that you can't meet them after all. Or the phone rings. You can probably see who's calling.

You have the power to say *yes* by taking the call, or to say *no* for now by letting it go to voicemail. That might seem like such an ordinary situation that it's not interesting. "Of course I have the power to take a call or let it go to voicemail!" But that's what I'm inviting you to do today... to notice the ordinary situations where you actually do exercise your right to set boundaries pretty well. So again, pause and feel what it's like to have that power, when the phone rings (or vibrates, or whatever yours does).

There are dozens of times a day when someone or something asks for permission to come into your space. When the phone rings... when an email arrives... when advertising appears... When you give your attention, you're saying *yes*. You also have the right to say *no*.

Today, your practice is to notice how it feels to say *yes* or *no* in all the ordinary little interactions that make up your day. When you say *yes*... and often you will... enjoy your power to choose *yes*. Notice if it feels different to read an email or answer a phone call, or have a conversation with a neighbor, having inwardly said a real *yes* to doing so.

Remember: Consciously exercise your power to say *Yes* **(and** *No***) in the ordinary interactions that make up your day.**

DAY 7

Creating Time And Space For Your Own Self

Taking time and space for your own self can be hard... unless you are good at boundaries.

How do you set a boundary when what you're guarding is your own time and space for self-care and play? Let's play with some options.

Remember whenever you say *no* to a request from someone, you're also saying *yes* to something else. You don't have to say this to the other person (remember a few days ago we talked about the power to say *no* without apologies or excuses?), but it's true.

Saying *no* to dinner with a friend is saying *yes* to the other thing you're planning to do that night. Saying *no* to the woman outside the grocery store collecting money for her cause, is saying *yes* to your right to choose something else to do with your money.

One of the hardest situations to say *no* in is when what you're saying *yes* to is purely for yourself, purely for your own time and space. Maybe you feel you have a right to say *no* to one person if you've committed to another person, or if you have to work, or if you're sick. But you might doubt your right to say *no* to a request if what you are saying *yes* to instead is yourself.

I think it's fascinating how this little boundaries question takes us to the really big questions, like "Do I have a right to be in this world?" and "Do I have as much value as anyone else?"

Wouldn't it be amazing to really feel and know that you DO have as much value as anyone else? If this is an issue for you, it's really worth taking time with.

The difference between you and other people is that you have primary responsibility for yourself. I always think of the saying, attributed to Hillel:

"If I am not for myself, who will be?"

We can't expect others to care for our needs if we're not taking responsibility for having those needs.

Yes, it would be nice if other people would intuit your needs without your ever having to know what they are! Then you wouldn't ever have to ask for anything and you'd never be rejected and you'd still get taken care of... Ha! Too bad it doesn't work that way.

For many years I did something I didn't really want to do because I didn't know how *not* to, and I didn't know I had the *right* not to. What was it?

It was hanging out with and interacting with the person I was living with.

As long as they were at home and awake, I felt I had to be with them, talking, eating together, watching TV... I vaguely felt like this was what people did, and I didn't even know the words I might've used to step away from that constant interaction and take some time for myself. As resentment and unease built up in me, I sometimes picked a fight or sniped at the person verbally. Sometimes I would even be aware of a longing to have some time and space to myself, but I wouldn't know what to do about it.

Then about 15 years ago, living with my current partner and my teenage daughter, I found myself saying one evening, "I need some introvert time."

My self-awareness had progressed to the point that I knew I wasn't rejecting them. I knew I wasn't breaking any rules. So I could say it calmly and not like I was picking a fight. And my announcement was accepted just as calmly! Sure, Ann needs some "introvert time"! Although I don't think I'm technically an introvert, I do think everyone needs introvert time, and that way of saying it really worked well for me and my family.

One thing I like about that way of saying it is that I was saying what I did want, and not what I didn't want. I didn't say, for example, "You two are driving me crazy, I have to get away from you." But introvert time, time by myself, was what I did want.

Let's pause for a moment so you can ask yourself: Is there somewhere in your life right now where you're doing something you don't really *want* to do out of a sense that you *have* to?

Yes, there are some things we more or less do have to do, such as taking care of living beings dependent on us. Although even in those cases there are probably more choices than we think.

But setting aside those cases, is there somewhere in your life right now where you feel a bit trapped or resentful but you don't feel you can do much about it? Let's pause to see if there's something like that for you.

And now ask yourself: *What would I want to be doing instead of that?* What is the *yes* you want to say to yourself if you said *no* to that?

I'm guessing what you want to say *yes* to is something for you... is that right?

Now pause and sense what comes when you say to yourself, internally, "I am a person of value, I have a right to be in this world, and that" - whatever that is in your example - "is something I get to say *yes* to for myself."

For example:

"I am a person of value, I have a right to be in this world, and spending time resting and reading is something I get to say *yes* to for myself."

Really give yourself some time to be aware of what comes!

You might feel an expansive sense of confidence and strength... solid ground... and... or... you might get in touch with something in you that doesn't believe you have this right, in which case you would turn toward it with compassion, put a gentle hand where you feel it, and say, "Hello I know you are there."

Great. So **for today, your practice is** to be aware of your own needs for yourself, for time for yourself, for space for yourself, and be aware whether you feel it's OK for you to hold these needs with at least equal value to the needs of others in your life. Just be aware.

If you discovered something in you that doesn't believe you have a right to create time and space for yourself, turn toward it with compassion. Bring a gentle hand to the place in your body where you feel it and say, "Hello, I know you're there." (If that part of you needs more company, see the Bonus Practice on the next page.)

Remember: You are a person of value, and you have a right to say *yes* to activities that are just for you.

For giving healing company to a part of you that isn't sure you have the right to be in the world

1. Pause and get grounded in your body. Feel your breathing.

2. Recall that YOU are the larger Self that includes all of you. Perhaps you could say the words, "I am the space where all my feelings can be as they are."

3. Bring awareness into the inner area of your body, your throat, chest, and stomach area.

4. Say (out loud or inwardly): "Perhaps there is something in me that isn't sure I have the right to be in the world."

5. Wait. The "something" that is afraid may come into your awareness slowly, and it may be a body feeling, an image, or even just a sense that something is there but hiding.

6. When the "something" comes, treat it gently. This is a "younger you." You might sense how they would like to be treated by you.

7. There is a healing presence in simply being there with this "younger you" who feels this way. There is no need to try to change its feelings. In fact, trying to change will hold back change. Just be there. Feel free to stop any time. Even short periods of this kind of inner company are valuable. And if it ever feels like too much, that is a trustworthy signal. You can stop and come back later.

8. If you feel any kind of shift in your body, like a deeper breath or a sense of release, take some time to enjoy that before stopping. You might also sense that this is something that wants you to return to it for more company. You can let it know you are willing to do that.

DAY 8

The Question Of How Much To Share

Today we'll practice how to assess how much information (personal, etc.) this particular situation needs.

T here's a kind of boundary we haven't talked about much, and it's a very interesting one. It's the boundary around how much we say, and how much information we share, especially personal information about ourselves.

Have you been aware that some people seem to "overshare"? They seem to share more information about themselves than the situation calls for, and perhaps you wonder why they do that.

Maybe you're someone who occasionally says more than you need to. If that is something you want to change, or want to have more choice over, let's work with that today.

Oversharing can slow things down, and it can actually interfere with getting our needs met, because the person we're talking to can get confused about what the main point is that we wanted to make.

I've talked before about Pausing. Pausing is a very powerful thing to do in any interaction. Pausing allows you to "gather" yourself... to get present in the situation... to feel what really matters to you here.

Before I learned to do Pausing I would sort of "blurt out" in many of my conversations. I would say things just because they were in my mind, without taking time to sense whether they were appropriate. Sometimes I'd step on people's toes, not literally, but with my words. I didn't know how to wait a moment before speaking to sense myself and what I really wanted to say.

I remember going with a friend of mine into a social situation. My friend had recently confided in me some personal details about her family. In those days, I didn't have healthy boundaries around what information was personal and what information wasn't mine to share. Plus, I tended to get anxious and embarrassed in social situations — which for some people means they get more quiet, but for me it meant the opposite. I talked more.

As I remember it, it was only when I became aware of the frozen look of horror on my friend's face that I realized I'd just told this whole group of people we didn't know very well all about my friend's personal family stuff. Like it was just something to be babbling on about.

When you bumble around enough, and enough people tell you that you hurt them when you said those tactless and inappropriate things, you start realizing that opening your mouth and letting anything come out is not a good idea!

Eventually I realized I needed to create a "reserve," like a waiting room or vestibule inside myself, where I could first sense what I wanted to say before saying it... and maybe decide not to say it, or to say it more briefly, or to say it in a way that fit the situation better. Pausing let me cultivate the ability to have that "reserve."

This also enabled me to be more articulate in even scarier situations like speaking up at big conferences. Standing up and blurting did not work there, believe me! But when I paused and sensed what I wanted to say, and let it form first inside of me, I actually sounded good when I spoke, and I saw people nodding and smiling.

So... are you someone who would benefit from a bit of practice in sensing before you speak? Let's have you give that a try today. This is not the same as "censorship" or not being spontaneous. It's simply taking a moment to be more present before we speak or act.

Your practice for today is pausing. Pausing before you speak in a meeting... Pausing before you hit SEND on an email... Pausing before you answer the question, "How are you?" And so on.

In that Pause, gather a sense of yourself in the present. And from what you feel and know, sense what part of that feels right to say.

By the way, if it's an email, check and be sure you said what you want the person to do in response, plainly and simply. That's so helpful for busy people! You're much more likely to get what you want. You're not censoring, you're editing!

Like many of our practices, this one gets easier over time. Let's just be curious what will happen today!

Remember: Pause before speaking or writing and gather what is really important and appropriate to say.

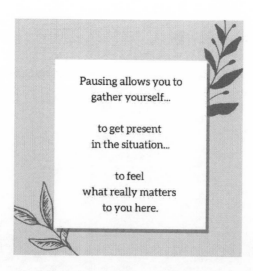

Pausing allows you to
gather yourself...

to get present
in the situation...

to feel
what really matters
to you here.

DAY 9

How Healthy Boundaries Help Us Connect Well With Others

Having healthy boundaries can open up
communication and forge
better channels of connection.

We're nine days into our healthy boundaries program, and perhaps it's about time to say what healthy boundaries ARE.

> A healthy boundary is not a rigid boundary that keeps everything out, and it's not a wide-open boundary that allows everything in. A healthy boundary keeps some things out and allows some things in... and has the wisdom to know the difference!

Your boundaries are flexible and change from time to time. They change with your state of energy and how much sleep you've gotten. They're different with different people. It doesn't work to set up fixed rules for our boundaries, does it? We need to sense freshly in each situation, because the situations are different... and we're different!

Tony Winiski, a cell biologist, reminds us that a cell membrane both protects the cell from what's outside it *and* connects the cell with what's outside it. A cell membrane is semipermeable, allowing in what nourishes the cell and filtering out what would hurt it. That's a great model for having healthy boundaries in living our lives. Especially that the cell membrane boundary not only protects, it also connects.

What I'd like us to reflect on today is how much having healthy boundaries is of benefit to the other people and the relationships in our lives. Being around a person with healthy boundaries is a great relief! Can you feel that?

Recently, I was visiting my friend Theres in Switzerland. I love having breakfast made by her! When she brought the toast to the table, she asked me, "How is it? Do you like it this way?" I had a look, I sensed inside, and I said, "Actually could it be a little darker?"

She cheerfully ran the toast through the toaster again. When we were sitting down and happily buttering our toast, she said to me, "It's so great the way you say what you want."

"You mean other people don't?" I asked her.

"They just say it's fine," Theres replied. "But sometimes I know it isn't. When you say what you want, it makes me so happy."

Can you sense where Theres is coming from? She could feel more relaxed with me because she knew if I needed something, I would say so. If I didn't like something, I would say so. With someone who was not so forthcoming, Theres felt she had to work harder, to draw it out of them or to guess what would make them happy as a guest.

Me too. I also love what happens when I'm around people who will speak up and let me know when something is missing or off or uncomfortable for them. Is it like that for you, too?

So... let's try something. Rather than thinking right now about our own healthy boundaries, let's take some time to sense how we like it when the other people in our lives have healthy boundaries.

What are the benefits for us when the other person knows what their boundaries are and states their needs clearly? Without anger or blaming or excuses? Just like, "Actually, could the toast be a little darker?"

I invite you to pause and get a sense of that.

Here are some things that might be coming up for you.

- You know where you stand.

- You can plan.

- You're not going to be confronted later with a resentful person who's mad at you for not guessing what they needed.

And what about closeness? Do you feel more connected to a person like that? If you know where you stand and the decks are clear, there can be a deep sense of connection.

I'd like to invite you to do a little process with me right now.

Take some time to get connected with your body... feel your breathing, and sense in the inner area of your body, your throat, chest, stomach, and so on. Just getting grounded and settled in yourself.

Remember what just came for you a minute ago – the possibility that with a person who has healthy boundaries, we can have a deep sense of connection.

Now, I invite you to become aware of an important person in your life, someone you're close to, and in your imagination put that person in front of you.

And now ask yourself: do I want to have that deep sense of connection with this person? Does it help me do that if I know what they need and what they like?

What would or does it feel like to have a deep sense of connection with this person? (Take some time...)

You can repeat this exercise with other people if you want to.

And one final part of the process: what would life be like if everyone you met all day had healthy boundaries? Just take a little time to imagine that!

One thing I find exciting about asking this kind of question is that it blows the myth that other people will hate it if I have healthy boundaries. That they'll be angry or critical. I'm not sure they will. Maybe they will love it! But we'll come back to that question in a few days and explore it some more.

Your practice for today is to notice those moments when other people in your life tell you honestly how they feel and what they want and how that impacts your feelings of closeness with them.

Remember: Notice how you feel when other people set clear and healthy boundaries with you.

DAY 10

The Hardest Person To Set A Boundary With

Who is your hardest person
to set a boundary with? Let's find out,
and also find out why.

Y esterday, I invited you to imagine an important person in your life and to sense what it would be like to have a deep sense of connection with them or to enjoy the deep sense of connection you already have.

Today, I invite you to think about the person in your life you have the hardest time setting boundaries with.

Did someone spring to mind already? For some of you, you already know who that person is. You might be thinking, "My mother," or "My son." Or the person you live with. Or your ex. You might already know who the hardest person is.

If you don't, this first question might need a bit of time. So let's take that time. Let's review the different people in your life...

Bring them into your awareness one by one... and ask yourself, "Is boundary-setting hard with this person?"

It might be members of your original family, whether you still live with them or not. Or, it might be the people or the person you live with.

But boundary setting can also be hard with friends, co-workers, members of your community, the salesperson in the clothing store... So who is it for you?

If it's difficult to choose between several people that feel about equally hard for you, then just pick one for now. You can always come back to the others and repeat the exercise later.

OK, so now you have one person who is hard to set boundaries with.

Now ask yourself: What's hard about setting boundaries with that person?

What is "something in you" worried will happen if you do set boundaries with that person? Maybe there is good reason to worry...

but the reason doesn't matter right now. Just take some time to
sense.

- Might "something in you" be worried the person will feel
  hurt? That they won't like you?

- Might it be worried the person will get angry and defensive?

- Might it be worried that you'll feel like you're guilty, or
  selfish, or insensitive?

Take some time to sense and acknowledge what you discover.

And then let it know you hear it.

We're going to come back to some of these issues in the following
sections.

But right now we're going to try something that's kind of fun. It's an
exercise I learned from Suzanne Slyman, called **Figure Eights**. Every
time I teach this to people, they love it.

We were talking yesterday about the way that healthy boundaries do
this wonderful job of both separating us AND connecting us with
other people. This exercise I'm about to show you is a way of vividly
picturing and experiencing this double function: separating AND
connecting.

Imagine that you're sitting in an empty room. I usually picture
myself sitting on the floor, but you could also put yourself in a chair.
In your mind, draw a circle around yourself, like on the floor around

you. Like a chalk circle, or a circle of light that goes completely around you.

Now bring that other person into your room. Put them a comfortable distance away, not too close, not too far. And draw a circle around them too, the same size as yours. Let the two circles be just touching.

Here's where the figure eights come in. Imagine that there's a line of light that moves around your circle, and then at the place where the two circles touch, it crosses over and moves around the other person's circle, and again at the touching point it moves back around your circle, and so on.

If you were looking from above you'd see the number 8. Two circles, connected at the touching point but also protected and bounded by this moving line of light. You can make the light any color. For some reason, mine is light blue.

Give yourself a few minutes to just let the light move around the circles.

And now let's check in. How is your feeling about the other person now?

Does it feel easier to be in their presence without worry and concern?

Does it feel more possible to feel them as a separate person with their own rights and yourself as a separate person with *your* own rights?

Just notice.

If anything about this exercise was hard, that can be something to get curious about. Or it might just be that you need to practice it a bit more! If it's really challenging to do the exercise with the person you chose, how about trying it with an easier person... and working up to the hard one.

Your practice for today... Think about a person you're likely to encounter who you find it hard to set boundaries with. And before you see the person, or get an email from them or a phone call, do the Figure Eights exercise with your inner picture of the person for 2-3 minutes. And then notice what happens!

Remember: With anyone who is extra hard to set a boundary with, visualize two circles of light around you and them that only touch at one point.

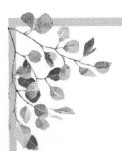

DAY 11

When Wanting People to Like You Stops You from Setting Boundaries

Will having no boundaries
make people like you?

Are you afraid that if you set clear boundaries and give clear messages about your needs, other people won't like you?

Or they'll be hurt and disappointed and that will drive a wedge between you?

If the answer is *yes*, at least some of the time, then your first step is to say, "Something in me is afraid that...." and fill in the rest of the sentence with your own words. Like: "Something in me is afraid that if I have clear boundaries, my friend will stop liking me."

The part of you that's afraid of losing connection with the other person because of setting a boundary is probably connected to a Younger You who might be feeling a more fundamental fear of not being welcome and not belonging in this world, just as you are.

I had so many issues with this growing up. I felt like an outsider in school. I was sharply aware of who the popular kids were and who were not. I was not.

I wanted to be liked, to be included, to belong and nothing I did — no way I changed myself — ever worked. Looking back now of course, it's pretty obvious that people can tell when you're trying to be liked... and they're put off by it.

D. H. Lawrence wrote: "The loveless never find love," and that's how it felt to me. I was missing something deep inside that I thought I could get from the popular kids — if I could just hit on the formula. But it was a fruitless quest.

What I really needed to do, and what I eventually did after Barbara McGavin and I developed Inner Relationship Focusing, was to turn toward that hurting one inside me who felt so loveless. So lacking in love.

There's a spiritual maxim that what we seek can be found inside us. Like in *The Wizard of Oz*, when Dorothy discovers she has always had the power to go home again. But if you're feeling loveless, you don't just go inside yourself and find love. It's not that easy. There's an additional step required.

That's what I'd like to take you through today. So let's do an exercise for being with that one in you who is longing to be liked, or to be loved, or to be included, or to belong...

Let's start with a situation where setting boundaries is challenging because something in you is afraid the other person won't like you if you're clear and direct about your boundaries.

Now use that language of "something in me is afraid that..." to acknowledge and name that part of you. Let awareness come into your body, and be open to feeling that part of you here now.

Let a fresh description come for how this "something in you" feels right now.

And let it know that you are here. Say, "I am here with you."

You already know this part of you wants to be liked. Take some time now to sense to a deeper level, to what it is longing for, or missing or lacking. Maybe what is lacking is a feeling of belonging, or of being held in unconditional love. Just take time to sense what that is from this part's point of view.

Give it your full compassion and empathy for that longing. So often we're shamed for these sort of longings. Like there's something wrong with us for wanting to be loved... Something that anyone would want!

So this now is the opposite of shaming. It's you giving this part of you full unconditional acceptance for how it feels. "Oh yes, I really get that you want that. Of course! No wonder! And I am here with you now."

Take some time to sense whether the younger part you're with can feel that you are there with it.

And this is the healing environment, the healing presence: that you are here with this Younger You, honoring and accepting exactly the way it feels.

This part of you may be showing you some memories of times of feeling unloved. If so, give empathy and compassion for that too. "I really get how hard that was and is for you."

What we seek can be found inside of us. And the steps that get us there are:

1. Looking inside you and connecting with the part of you that's missing something, lacking something, longing for something.

2. Creating a compassionate relationship with that part.

3. Completely accepting its need.

When you can do these things, what has been missing is being supplied.

It's not what you find inside but how you treat it when you find it that makes all the difference.

Your practice for today is to periodically visit and spend time with the Younger You who is concerned about whether other people like it... and just keep on experiencing that healing inner relationship.

Remember: There's nothing wrong with wanting to be loved! AND you can still have healthy boundaries.

DAY 12

Saying No Without Feeling Guilty Or Selfish

Are you being selfish if you set a boundary?

Would you feel guilty if you didn't give in to the requests of people close to you?

The trouble is, questions like, "Am I being selfish?" or, "Should I feel guilty?" are loaded questions. It's hard to answer them because they're full of assumptions. It might be more productive to question those assumptions!

Is there such a thing as "selfish"? How would we define it?

What do "guilt" feelings do for us? Do they help us live in accord with our values, or are they just another way to feel bad?

In my experience, feeling "guilty" or "selfish" is usually a sign that a part of you is afraid you'll get attacked by others for your choices.

Let's start with the concept of being "selfish." I put quotes around it because I think "selfish" is one of those words that can mean very different things depending on who uses it and the intention and purpose of the person who uses it.

If you're someone who finds yourself worrying you'll *be* selfish or you'll be *considered* selfish by others (which is not exactly the same thing!), then our first question has to be: what does "selfish" mean to you? How would you rephrase "selfish" using other words?

Let me put that another way: When you don't want to be "selfish," what is it that you're *not* wanting to be?

Maybe you define "selfish" as being oblivious to the needs of others.

Or maybe you define "selfish" as putting a much higher value on your own needs compared to the needs of others.

Or do you define "selfish" as paying any attention to your own needs?

Or maybe it's when your attention to your needs gets out of balance that you feel concerned?

Or maybe your worry is not that you'd be selfish if you set some boundaries, but that you'd be *called* selfish. That other people, and especially the person you're setting the boundary with, would consider you selfish.

The problem there is, people tend to call other people "selfish" to try to get them to do things. In those cases, it's not so much the meaning of the word as it is that "selfish" is being used as a lever to try to control someone's behavior.

My friend June visits her elderly mother in the care home every day. One day she wanted to go to a seminar for her own development, so she arranged for a friend to visit her mother and make sure she was OK. The next day, June's mother accused June of being selfish for not coming to see her. You tell me: was June selfish? We wouldn't say so, would we?

But it hurt June to be called selfish by her mother. June wants her mother to be happy and she wants her mother to appreciate her efforts. That's a tough spot to be in, with a mother who calls you selfish as a way to manipulate your actions.

Remember earlier we talked about how confusing it can be when people make indirect requests? Being called "selfish" by another person can be seen as an indirect request. When you hear it, you can say to yourself — even if it doesn't feel possible to say it to the other person — "What is this person requesting from me?"

June realized that when her mother called her selfish, she was requesting that June visit in person every day. Recognizing the unspoken request allowed June to be clear that she wasn't selfish for wanting a day off now and then. Not at all.

June still longs for her mother to really appreciate her efforts. But it's clearer to her that going to visit her mother every day, and fulfilling her mother's other needs as well, is not getting her any closer to being appreciated. Maybe she can try to get that need met more directly. Perhaps by initiating a conversation with her mother about what they appreciate about each other. No guarantee that'll work either. But at least it will get her away from the unhelpful question "Am I being selfish?"

Is there a place in your life, in your relationships, in your boundary setting, where you wonder whether you'd be selfish if you said no to a certain request? Or if you took some time for yourself?

Think about some of your key relationships...

What you do for the other person/people; whether you get to take some time off or pursue your own activities...

Does the question "Am I being selfish?" or "Should I feel guilty?" ever come up for you?

Have you got an example?

OK, now let's shift the question. In that same situation, instead of "Am I being selfish?" try asking, "What would be in accord with my values?"

Knowing what you value isn't just a mental exercise. Your values are principles by which you live your life. You determine them — and you can choose to live with them and by them.

Being in touch with your own values gives you a touchstone you can consult when faced with a decision, such as whether to say *yes* or *no* to a request by a close friend or family member.

For example, my friend Dina asked me if I would drive her to a medical procedure, and then drive her home. It was inconvenient for me. I'd have to reschedule some appointments. But when I consulted my values, I could feel the inner rightness of taking Dina to her appointment. She's a very close friend and I value the way she and I can ask each other for help and support like this. Saying *yes* to this request, despite its inconvenience, helps me live the kind of life I want to live.

Consulting my values helped me feel confident about my response to my friend. Asking myself, "Am I being selfish" or "Should I feel guilty?" wouldn't have gotten me the same result.

Your practice for today is to be curious about what question you'd prefer to ask, when the issue of being selfish or feeling guilty comes up.

Notice today any moment when your thoughts bring up the question of whether you — or anyone else — is being selfish. And then wonder: By what set of values do I want to answer that question?

And perhaps the question "Am I being selfish or not?" will become "Is this in accord with my values or not?"

Remember: You have a right to determine the values you will live by.

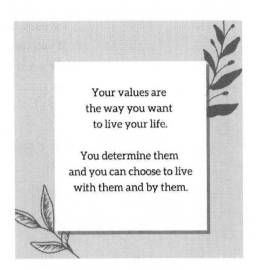

Your values are
the way you want
to live your life.

You determine them
and you can choose to live
with them and by them.

DAY 13

Standing Your Ground When the Other Person is Angry or Critical

The other person has a right to their feelings as
much as you do to yours.
Here's how to be OK with this.

When you consider daring to set boundaries with another person, one of the things that may stop you is a fear of the other person being angry or critical.

And they might. They do have a right to their own feelings.

On the other hand, other people's anger can be scary. So let's unpack some of the different factors involved.

First of all, if you're in actual physical danger from the anger of another person, please take steps to get yourself safe. My other tips might not apply to you if your actual safety is at issue.

Another factor might be *how* you're asserting your boundary.

If you have to work yourself into feeling angry or blaming the other person in order to set a boundary, then no wonder the other person would react the same way. We worked on this issue on Day Three. You might want to have a look at my PDF called Kind Ways to Say No. You can find it on the resource page I've created for you here: https://focusingresources.com/hbmore.

Just to be clear, I'm not saying that you're causing the other person's anger. Let's just be sure we're not triggering it unnecessarily!

So assuming you're not angry or blaming, that you're in touch with how setting this boundary fits with your needs and your values, and you're at peace with all that... the other person still might have an angry, blaming, critical reaction.

Now let me offer you a powerful reframe for that other person's angry, critical reaction. They probably react that way because they're scared.

People can get scared when how-it-has-always-been is threatened, when their source of something they feel they need might be taken away, when they feel their control of the situation slipping away.

And they can also get scared when they feel rejected and unloved. Not giving the other person what they want shouldn't mean that you don't love them, but to some younger part inside them, it might feel that way.

Does that make sense? If someone feels scared and hurt but doesn't want to show they feel vulnerable, they're going to lash out with anger. Of course that's a part of them, not their whole wise Self.

So another way to say this is, when we feel scared, hurt, and vulnerable but don't want to show it, we can get taken over by an angry part of us.

Let me show you what I mean by having you imagine a person in your life — someone you're close to who could get angry if you say No to something they want from you. Maybe they've gotten angry in the past, or maybe you've been holding back from setting a boundary with them for fear they'll get angry.

If there's not an actual person who comes to mind, you can imagine a vague anonymous person... just "someone." OK?

Now in your imagination, put yourself in a scenario where you draw your line, you say you're not going to be able to keep doing something for them, or whatever it might be in this case.

And imagine their reaction.

Now we're going to freeze time (because this is our imagination, so we can do whatever we want) and just empathize with that person in our minds. Did you imagine an angry reaction?

If you have a part of you that already cringed and ducked, just put a gentle arm around that scared part of you, and let it know you are here.

The scared part of you has your arm around it, and the Big You can look at the other person and their angry reaction, and just feel into this question: Might they actually be scared?

Might their anger be coming from feeling hurt and vulnerable? Might they feel that something precious to them has been threatened?

Just pause and sense into that.

And if you do sense that there's vulnerability under that anger, notice if that makes it easier for you to be there, to stand your ground.

Let's change our scenario a little. Same situation: you're drawing your line, setting your boundary with this person. But this time, imagine the person is able to get in touch with how they truly feel, and they feel safe enough to share that with you. Imagine them saying something like, "I felt scared when you said that... something in me felt scared. I guess I'm scared about losing my connection with you..." — and so on. What else might they say?

That's a lot easier to hear, right? Do you feel your heart opening up to that person? Of course! And you can still set your boundary! But you can tell the person it doesn't mean they're going to lose you or whatever else would be true from your heart.

It is a lot easier to hear the other person's more vulnerable feelings than it is to hear their anger. Right?

So the idea here is that when you set your boundary and you get back anger, you can empathically imagine the scared, vulnerable feeling behind the other person's anger and that makes it easier to take. And easier to stand your ground.

Today your practice is to notice if there are times when you'd like to set a boundary but you hold back for fear of the other person's anger... and then get curious about whether it helps to remember that anger in the face of someone setting a boundary is probably really something vulnerable and scared.

Remember: The other person has a right to their feelings AND you have a right to stand your ground.

The thought of another person's anger can be frightening. Here's a way to help with that.

1. Pause and get grounded in your body. Feel your breathing.

2. Recall that YOU are the larger Self that includes all of you. Perhaps you could say the words, "I am the space where all my feelings can be as they are."

3. Bring awareness into the inner area of your body, your throat, chest, and stomach area.

4. Gently invite a part of you that is scared of the other person's anger, to come into your awareness now.

5. Wait. The "something" that's scared may come into your awareness slowly, and it may be a body feeling, an image, or even just a sense that something is there but hiding.

6. When the "something" comes, be gentle. If it's a body

feeling, you might let a gentle hand go to the place where you feel it.

7. There's a healing presence in simply being there with this part of you that's scared. Let it know you know it's there... and you are with it.

8. What might happen is that you get shown images and memories that help you understand why this part of you would be so scared of another person's anger. Accept and validate the memory by saying, "I see what you're showing me, and no wonder you'd be scared, if you're afraid that could happen again."

This is all you need to do. Give this all the time it needs to feel heard.

If you feel any kind of shift in your body, like a deeper breath or a sense of release, take some time to enjoy that before stopping.

You might also sense that this is something that wants you to return to it for more company. You can let it know you're willing to do that.

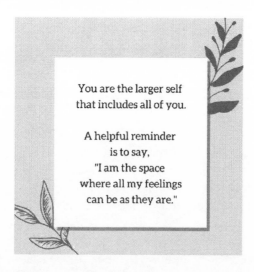

You are the larger self
that includes all of you.

A helpful reminder
is to say,
"I am the space
where all my feelings
can be as they are."

DAY 14

When Your Trauma History Is Involved

Boundary issues can be even more challenging than they would otherwise be when our own trauma history is involved.

C urrent life situations can carry the shadow of past unhealed trauma. Let's find out some healing steps you can take when that happens.

By trauma I simply mean that if hard things happened to you in the past, usually when you were a child, and if there was no possibility for healing or resolution at the time, then there's a part of you that stays frozen in the hard time and reacts to present events as if they're what happened back then.

This is a broader definition of trauma than many people use. I like it, because it lets us see that anything that consistently blocks the life forward energy of a person, and doesn't allow important needs to be met, has a very similar effect. The effect is a kind of freezing of the one who went through it, as if that one is still here, still going through it.

The good news is that this blocked life forward energy can resume. The frozenness of the trauma state can unfreeze. The healing and resolution that didn't happen then can happen now. It's not too late.

If as a child you were disrespected, or shamed, or not allowed to have your own wants and feelings, and this happened repeatedly and consistently, and there was no one to talk to about it to get empathy and compassion, then you have a trauma history. This can make boundary setting harder.

But if you look at it the other way — and this is the way I like to look at it! — the challenges that come from boundary setting can help you discover these unhealed places from the past. And now they can be given company and enabled to release and move forward again. Wow, that's a great thing!

All through this book I've been showing you how to turn toward and be with your emotional states. On Day One I pointed out that the most important boundary to set first is between being *identified* with your emotions and being able to *be with* your emotions.

This ability to be larger than your emotions is called being Self-in-Presence. You — as Self-in-Presence — are the healing environment for the hurt younger self inside you. And you don't have to feel particularly strong or stable in order to do that! You just need to be present.

When we worked with the fear of being abandoned and alone, with not setting boundaries because of wanting people to like you, and other issues in this book, you've practiced turning toward and being with a "younger you" inside.

I use the phrase "younger you" instead of "inner child" for two reasons. For one, it may not be a child. The hard things that happened to you might have been in your 20s or 30s. (Really, at any age earlier than now.) And the phrase "inner child" carries the idea of some permanently childlike part of us. But the "younger you" who's frozen in the earlier hard time is not permanent. When what was missing is supplied, the frozenness can release and life moves forward again.

Even though the hard things that happened might have been later than childhood and might not have involved your parents, your life with your parents still impacts your sense of your right to set boundaries and have your needs respected.

Your parents' abilities or lack of ability to have healthy boundaries and respect the boundaries of others would have a big impact on you, of course.

So let's do a little process where you spend some time with the Younger You who experienced life with your parents.

Take some time to get grounded in your body. Feel the support of what you're sitting on, knowing you can rest into that support and it will hold you. Feeling your breathing and the inner area of your body, your throat, chest, stomach, that whole inner area.

In you now there is a Younger You who was affected by growing up with your parents, by their ability to respect boundaries, by their ability to regulate their emotions, by their commitment or lack of commitment to keeping you physically safe. (And if it's not your parents who come to mind but someone else, like your siblings, that's OK, feel free to adapt this process so it fits your circumstance.)

What I'm inviting you to do is to sit down quietly with the Younger You who went through all that. Maybe feeling in your body the place where it is right now... and letting a gentle hand go there, like you're saying "I am with you."

Let it show you what they went through, show you inner home movies of things that happened that were hard.

And you say, "I see what you're showing me, and I get how really hard that was and still is, for you."

The showing of the home movies, and someone who can bear witness to what happened and that it was really hard, is a healing process. You'll probably find that the Younger You gets more relaxed and feels safer as you go along. Just notice.

If this process needs more time, feel free to take that time.

In fact, this is **your practice for today:** To be in an inner contact with the Younger You who went through hard times, and to say to it, "Yes, I see what you went through, and I see that wasn't right, and I am here now."

Remember: If your current life is impacted by hard things that happened to you in the past, you can spend time today with that younger part of you and that makes a difference.

DAY 15

Separating the Other Person's Feelings from Your Own

Boundary issues can be even more challenging than they would otherwise be when our own trauma history is involved.

W e've talked as if setting boundaries is always a case of saying *yes* or *no*. Knowing you have a right to your own needs and being able to discover what request the other person is making... all of these are important abilities to practice.

But there's another kind of boundary issue, and that's the boundary between me and you, my feelings and your feelings.

Do you find yourself picking up other people's feelings in your body? Do you feel like the boundary you really need to work on is the boundary between other people's feelings and you?

The times when we pick up other people's feelings most easily is when they are not owning their feelings. It's as if feelings that aren't being owned and acknowledged leak out and sort of fly around the room, glomming onto anyone! But if the person can acknowledge their feelings, that puts an inner boundary around them where they don't fly out and invade other people.

Hidden, unacknowledged, unowned emotions tend to get picked up much more easily. It's not how strong the feelings are, it's whether they're owned and acknowledged by the person they belong to.

Interestingly, it doesn't seem to matter if the person acknowledges the feelings out loud or just does it silently. The effect on the other people in the room is still that the feelings are contained by the person who has them.

This is another super-good reason to practice being Self-in-Presence! When we can be present for our own feelings, we're being responsible toward other people as well as to ourselves.

But what can you do if you are picking up other people's feelings? No matter how much you develop your own Self-in-Presence, this still might happen.

It can help to inwardly acknowledge your feelings as yours, and their feelings as theirs. Let me take you through a little process to show you what I mean.

Take a little time to get centered in your body, to feel your contact on what you are sitting on. Feel your breathing and the inner area of your body.

Now remember a time when you were with someone who evidently had a feeling. You could tell from the nonverbal cues, maybe the intensity of the voice, that there was some feeling there, but the person wasn't saying so. The person wasn't saying, "I am feeling this" or "something in me is feeling this."

And now, as you listen to that person in your imagination, do two things inwardly. No need to say these things out loud, just inwardly.

ONE: Be aware of your own feelings.

Say to yourself, "I am sensing how I am feeling right now... and I am acknowledging that."

TWO: Make a guess about the other person's feelings.

Say to yourself, "I am guessing that this person is feeling _____ right now."

Now move back to your own feelings and notice that they're different from how you're guessing the other person is feeling. Of course they are. (If it seems at first that the feelings of both people are the same -- like "They are angry, and I am angry" -- delve a little deeper. What's the quality of your anger? The quality of their anger? At some level they are different.)

Once you're aware of your feeling and your guess about their feeling, you can say inwardly, "This is me, and this is you."

If you like, and if it fits the situation, you can also imagine an empathic statement to the other person, like, "I'm guessing this is pretty hard for you." When I say "I'm guessing" to another person, it also reminds me that this is their feeling, not mine.

How did you feel about this imagination exercise? What did it bring up for you? Something there might need some more company!

Your practice for today: The next time you're having a conversation with someone, in person or remotely, do this "double acknowledging." This is how I'm feeling, and this is how I'm guessing you're feeling. If appropriate, let the person know how you're feeling. Notice what happens.

Remember: Inwardly say, "This is how I feel, and this is how I'm guessing you feel."

DAY 16

How Introverts Can Set Boundaries

Boundary issues can be even more challenging than they would otherwise be when our own trauma history is involved.

Is it harder to set boundaries if you are an introvert? Maybe... maybe not.

People think that introverts are shy, but shyness is something else. Extroverts can be shy, and introverts might not be shy. What looks like an introvert being shy is actually an introvert being quiet.

Introverts tend to be more quiet and reserved. They know about turning inward, and are good at it. They tend to have an easier time being self-aware.

So the part of setting boundaries that involves knowing yourself and being in touch with what you feel and want is definitely easier for introverts.

But the part that involves speaking up, being assertive, might be harder.

Do we have to be assertive to set a boundary? Do we even have to speak to another person? Not necessarily.

Sometimes the inner act of knowing that we draw the line can be enough to change the outer situation. I don't pretend to know how this works, but I've seen it happen a number of times. A person comes to an inner clarity, "No, I can't take this any more, if my spouse/partner/friend does this one more time, I'm going to say clearly that it's not OK." And then the other person never does it again!

I'm convinced that the more we deeply know, with confidence, what we need, and the more we know we have a right to our own time, our own space, to get respect, etc., the more we find ourselves communicating about it with our posture, our tone, our mood – nonverbally.

Closing a door to a room can set a boundary. Opening a book and starting to read can end a conversation. Once we're clear, there are many ways to communicate about it. I have a friend who is good at growling when his boundary is crossed. He doesn't like to share personal information, and sometimes I forget that about him. "Have you been writing lately?" I'll ask him. "Grr-r-r-r-r-r." Oh, OK. Now I remember.

Inner clarity that something has crossed our boundary is so important and may be all we need. But not always. The nonverbal doesn't always work. I think we need to be ready to back up our nonverbal with verbal. Some people don't pick up subtlety.

My favorite way of communicating about my boundaries with another person is to assume they don't know what my boundaries are, and that they would want to know. By telling them I need something different from what's going on, I'm giving them information they'd want to have.

I know this isn't always true! But it's a philosophy of mine, and it seems to work very well. Start by assuming good intentions. Communicate first from that assumption. And then go forward from there.

My partner is a writer and doesn't like to talk about the book he is writing right now. We share a personal trainer, a friendly guy who makes conversation while taking you through the strength training. The other day J. complained to me that N. is intrusive and annoying. "Really?" I said, "What does he do?" "He's always asking me how my current book is going." "And did you ask him to not ask you that?" "No... That would be rude."

So J. is stuck with complaining to me that N. is intrusive and annoying, because telling N. that he'd rather not talk about his current book would be rude! I said to J, "He doesn't want to annoy you! He has no idea that talking about your current book is something you don't want to do... unless you tell him!"

That's a great example of what I mean about assuming the other person would want to know. The long-term health of any relationship can depend on getting clear about what crosses our boundaries.

Let's do a little imagination exercise that may help with this. Your actual relationships may be complex in ways I can't predict, so I invite you to imagine you've made a new friend. You're getting to know this person, you've had a few lunches, and so far so good, you're compatible and enjoy each others' company.

But now the person is starting to feel a bit distant. They're not returning your calls right away. When you do get together, it's not clicking the way it used to. This promising friendship might fade away.

Now imagine you could read that person's mind. And what's going on in there is that "so-and-so" — you — "has got this intrusive habit of asking me about my (fill in the blank) and speaking up about it would be rude and wouldn't do any good, so I'm just withdrawing."

I mean, to me, ending a relationship because you haven't dared to be "rude" is like trading in your car because the ashtrays are full! It just doesn't seem in proportion.

Anyway, you've peeked into the mind of your new friend, and you saw what was going on. Now take a moment to get in touch with how much you'd welcome hearing whatever it is about you that's been bothering them. Just that much. Your own inner feeling of welcome.

If you're like me, you probably feel you'd much prefer the person to speak up than to withdraw. We really don't know each other. If we're introverts, it's even harder to know what goes on inside! So informing each other calmly about something that could affect the relationship if not addressed is a really good idea.

Anyway, back to how introverts set boundaries. Often: non-verbally. If necessary, verbally. Because sometimes other people can't guess how you feel!

Your practice for today: Be curious about the people you encounter in your day. Wonder about the ways their wishes and needs might be different from yours. See if it feels true that if there is some way they are stepping on your toes, they would probably like to know. And then see what happens.

Remember: If you're clear inwardly about what your boundaries are, you may not have to say them out loud. But if necessary, state them calmly and simply.

DAY 17

When People Are Really Intrusive

It makes sense that you wouldn't want to be pushed into doing what someone else wants. It even makes sense to be angry about it!

W e've talked about how tricky it can be to set a boundary when the person only hints at what they want, and never comes out and asks directly.

But the opposite can also be a problem — when the person insists and persists and demands, and generally behaves as if it is not an option for you to say *no*. Because the very way this person is behaving is already crossing a boundary.

The panhandler who knocks on your car window to ask for money has already violated your space. The family member who insists you take time to hear her argument that she needs to borrow your car has already taken up your time without your permission.

And you know what? It makes sense to be angry about this kind of thing. In fact, I want to talk today about healthy outrage.

You might have grown up in a setting where it was not OK to be angry, even when someone did something outrageous. You can give healing compassion to the Younger You who had their boundaries violated and then wasn't allowed to feel their upset, fear, and anger in response. And you can cultivate your ability to feel your outrage when it happens now. If forceful anger is appropriate to this situation, then it could be the best thing to do.

A story comes to mind from my grad school days in Chicago. I was walking along the street, and nobody else was around until a young man, a stranger, came up to me from behind and whispered something sexually explicit in my ear. OUTRAGE flooded my body and I turned around and stamped on the ground toward him, saying, "Beat it! Get out of here!"

I don't know where that outrage came from because it happened before I could think, but it turned out to be the perfect thing to do. The guy melted away like snow on a hot day! And I felt so empowered.

We've talked about how it's not necessary to work yourself up into anger in order to set a boundary. And that's true. You can communicate about your boundary calmly and with the assumption that you have a right to set it. You can start with the assumption the other person is of good will and wants to know what you want and need, as we talked about in the last section.

But there are also those times when what the other person is doing is truly violating and intrusive. And then you get to be angry about it. You get to let your outrage show in your voice because that's appropriate to the situation.

Sarcasm is another move that might be appropriate if the other person needs to be stopped in their tracks. I love the expression, "What part of *no* do you not understand?" I haven't had to use it very often... but I really like having it in my repertoire. If I used it, it would come only after a conversation where many milder requests have gone unheeded, and the person was still being intrusive.

If you don't like being sarcastic, here's a kinder way to give the same message: "I don't know if you noticed that I already said no to that."

Let's do an exercise connected to feeling healthy outrage. Are you ready?

Take some time to get centered and settle into your body. And now imagine you've been given full permission to get angry when something happens that violates your boundaries or the boundaries of someone vulnerable who you're protecting.

Notice I'm not saying you have to get angry, or that you should get angry. Just that you *can*. It's permitted. You have that right.

Now cast your mind back to one or more incidents where something happened that was clearly wrong. It was unfair, unjust, or violating of someone's right to integrity. Let's pause a moment and let you recall something like that.

Yes, it's OK if it's something you read about or saw in a video. As long as you can imagine it, it will work for our exercise.

Let it play out, watch the scene and feel in your body with your permission now to get angry, if it makes you angry. And if not angry, notice what you do feel. I think we have an inner sense of rightness, an inner sense of justice and fairness — although of course it's somewhat different for different people.

You might also notice whether it feels like there's something from your own history that makes it harder for you to tell whether the scene playing in front of you is really something violating and wrong, and whether it's hard for you to have your genuine feelings in response to it.

Your practice for today... Notice if something you experience or see or hear about today brings up your sense of healthy outrage. Remembering that healthy outrage is a kind of anger that comes out of protectiveness toward the more vulnerable among us. And then notice how it feels to allow yourself to feel that. Just as it is.

Feeling anger is not the same as expressing anger. Be sure to pause and collect your sense of

Self-in-Presence before speaking and taking action on your healthy outrage, in order to ensure that you and others are protected. And then do act.

Remember: You have a right to feel outrage when the rights of the vulnerable are violated, including your own.

DAY 18

Setting Boundaries With Yourself

Do you have an inner driver who won't let you rest? Let's find out how to set boundaries with that one.

Boundary setting isn't something we only need to do in our relationships with other people. We also need to set boundaries within ourselves.

I'm thinking especially about the times when there's a part of you pushing you to work harder — a part that seemingly has disdain for any activity that isn't "productive."

This part will try to make you feel guilty for taking time for play, rest, enjoying nature and beauty, and companionship... "You haven't accomplished enough to be taking time off!" it says.

To this part of us, only work, achievement, and duty are important. Anything else is "taking time off" or "goofing off." Do you have a part of you like that?

If a part of you believes only work and duty are important, and it shames you when you take time off, or when you go for what gives you pleasure and joy, that's an anxious part. There's another part who feels ashamed and guilty at taking any time off for pleasure and joy, and works hard to try to meet the standards of the anxious one.

Of course, this pattern is not healthy or sustainable. Sure, you might get a lot done, but without a feeling of real satisfaction because to that inner pushing part, nothing is ever enough. And the hard-working part of you will become more and more exhausted until the result is some kind of breakdown, even illness or accident. Sometimes there's also an addiction that allows the pattern to keep going — like working too hard in the daytime, overindulging at night — but to the detriment of your health and well-being.

How do we shift this? Start with: "Something in me feels guilty if I take time to give myself pleasure and joy." (Change those words if you need to, to fit you better.)

Take some time to pause. Get grounded in your body. Now invite this part of you into your awareness. You might see an image of it, feel it in your body, or be aware of it in the room somewhere, possibly hiding.

Give that part of you a gentle acknowledgement, like you're saying, "Hello I know you're there."

And then get in touch with how it's doing. Is it exhausted? Downtrodden? Resentful? Longing? Or something else that might be hard to describe?

This is a part you might often feel identified with... in other words, you might feel that you are the one that feels guilty and exhausted... or whatever.

So it's a big step to be able to say that "something in you" feels this way and then to give that part of you some gentle company. Maybe let a gentle hand go there, where you feel it.

And now let's turn toward another part of you that we're guessing is probably there as well.

If there's a part feeling guilty at taking time for pleasure and joy (or whatever your words were), then there's probably another part that is making it feel guilty. Whether or not you can hear words in your head like, "You should only do things that are productive and useful," we're going to assume there's a part of you pushing that point of view. (It might even be saying you don't deserve to take time off.)

We're also going to assume that this part is anxious. It may sound mean or stern or even angry, but I can assure you that its basic motivation is anxiety. In other words, it's worried.

So take a moment to say an inner Hello to a part of you that's pushing you to work hard and not take time off, especially not for pleasure and joy.

As you say Hello to it, see if you can locate it... slightly behind your right ear, or over on your left, or in your head... it's around here somewhere. This kind of part might not have a body feeling but you can still get a feel for its mood.

See if you can sense that it's worried about you and that's why it is pushing and guilt-tripping you (or another something in you).

Remember — *you* are not the one feeling guilty! You already said hello to that *part* of you. Maybe your hand is still there with it.

So the you that's turning toward this anxious pushing part of you is not the one who feels guilty, it's the Big You, the one we call Self-in-Presence.

From your Big Self, offer some compassion to this anxious part of you. Let it know you hear how worried it is about the bad things that will happen to you if you take time off for pleasure and joy. In acknowledging its worry, you don't have to agree or disagree. It doesn't matter if it is right or wrong. What matters is that it can feel you care about its concerns.

You see, ideally the actions in our lives would not spring from our parts. It would be we ourselves, not our parts, that decide and act in our lives. When all goes smoothly, we don't have to tell ourselves what to do. We simply take grounded action that is appropriate to what we want and need.

Your practice for today: Notice if there is a part of you judging how you're spending your time. And then rather than arguing, say to that judging part, "Might you be worried about something?"

When you can acknowledge a part of you that's pushing your behavior out of anxiety, it loses its power to make you feel bad and it starts to relax, because it can feel that you are here, ready to make wise choices. This shift might not happen instantly, but every time we say Hello to a worried part, we are moving in this direction.

Remember: You can turn toward any self-judging part of you, and say "Might you be worried about something?"

DAY 19

How To Lovingly Connect Without Giving Up On Your Needs

Setting boundaries can be done with love.
Let's explore how.

C an you set a boundary with love? Is knowing and honoring your own needs consistent with loving someone?

I hope by now you agree with me that the answer is Yes!

We've talked about how to be with parts of us that might fear the other person's anger or abandonment if we set a clear boundary with them. Fearing abandonment might *feel* like love (to a part of us), but it's not. It's what we used to call, in the 60s, being "hung up"! I guess now it would be called codependency, or having attachment issues.

Take a moment to ask yourself whether you feel confident about being able to set boundaries with love, or whether that's still a shaky area for you.

For some of us, there may be a seesaw between a part that feels, "I have to give in to the person (or stay silent) because I'm afraid they will leave me if I don't..." and another part that feels, "I have to harden my heart and not care about them before I can take care of my own needs." It seems like I have to choose one or the other.

But I don't. There's a middle ground, a place where I can have me, you can have you, and we can meet.

Many years ago — when trying to shift out of the messy boundaries in my marriage — I coined the phrase "Good Boundaries with an Open Heart." At the time, for me, that was an impossible goal. I felt like in order to set a boundary that honored my needs, I had to close my heart to the other person. I could not both feel my love for them *and* be clear that I would not do what they were asking, or that I would not put up with their behavior. Good boundaries with an open heart was almost an oxymoron, two concepts in one sentence that are impossible to have at the same time.

But I learned it was possible to hold a loving intention toward the other person and set my boundary. Now it's not hard for me at all.

And that comes with an understanding that it's not just whether I set a boundary, it's also how I do it.

Today I was in line at the supermarket behind a woman with two young kids. One of the kids reached for the brightly colored lollipops that the supermarket put out at the checkout line. "Mommy, can we get that?"

The mom said calmly, "That looks nice, doesn't it? We're not going to get that today." I loved how she handled that. "That looks nice, doesn't it?" acknowledged the child's point of view. Then "We're not going to get that today," was her own boundary. And doing it calmly, without drama, was also a communication, a sort of underlying, "We are OK" message.

Giving the other person empathy is not the same as giving in on my point of view. "I see how it is for you." "I see why you'd want that." "I understand where you're coming from."

These empathic statements are not the same as agreement. I am not giving in or giving up when I understand where you are coming from.

But I might be moved! Being open to being moved by the other is a loving act. I might say, "Now that you tell me how much this means to you, I'm starting to feel differently about it." I've learned I can trust my inner sense of rightness, I can trust my sense of being moved by the other person's story.

In the old days, when I didn't feel confident in my right to say *no* or *yes*, I couldn't trust that the sense of being moved wasn't my own parts tricking me into giving in. Now I can.

Confidence that I can say *no* or *yes* gives me a lot of inner spaciousness. It gives me room to be generous without feeling like I am losing something.

Let's explore this.

I want you to pick someone you love, and they love you. For the purpose of this exercise pick a relationship in your life that has the least complications. Maybe a friend... or your favorite family member... your Focusing partner... it can even be someone no longer living, because this is going to be an imaginary conversation. We want the person with whom there is the least drama.

And now create a meeting with this person, maybe at a cafe or in a comfortable room. You are both relaxed, nobody is in a hurry. Take some time to feel your enjoyment at this simple, warm connection.

Now your friend says they want to ask you a favor.

Notice if you are open to hearing what the favor is... and assuming that you are, take some time to sense what it feels like to be open to hearing what the favor is, and yet at the same time knowing you have the right to say *yes* or *no*.

The essence of the exercise is:

1. The person asks you if they can ask you a favor, and you check inside.

2. You can feel at the same time your willingness to hear what the favor is, and your own confidence in your right to say *yes* or *no*.

3. Oh, and let's not forget that you love this person.

Notice how it feels to hold this person in loving regard and at the same time know that you have the right to say *yes* or *no* to the favor they're asking.

Sure, there might be other people in your life with whom this would be more difficult! The reason I wanted you to do this exercise with the easiest person you can think of is to help you practice what it feels like to have good boundaries with an open heart. Being able to feel what this is like becomes a template and a resource for other situations and other people.

Your practice for today is to hold in your heart and your body what it feels like to love someone with an open heart and know you have a right to your own needs. Just walk around that way. And be aware and curious.

Remember: You can love someone and say *yes* or *no* when they ask you for something. Without closing off your heart.

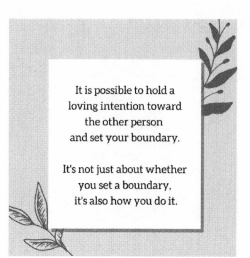

It is possible to hold a
loving intention toward
the other person
and set your boundary.

It's not just about whether
you set a boundary,
it's also how you do it.

DAY 20

Experiencing Yourself As A Separate Being From Others

We are all both interconnected and separate.
The art is in the balance between the two.

Y ou've explored the boundaries between you and other people in a number of different ways. You've done the Figure Eight exercise that lets you practice feeling yourself as both connected and separate from another person. You've experienced holding the other person in loving regard while still being able to honor your own needs. You've touched on the possibility of standing your ground even when someone is angry with you for setting a boundary and also the possibility of having your own healthy outrage when a boundary is violated. And we've talked about how it's sometimes hard to separate other people's feelings from your own.

In all of this, one key issue is this: Simply being who you are in the presence of another person.

Being in the presence of another person is a different experience from being alone. I remember when I couldn't tell how I felt if I was with another person. It was like the other person's "field" was so big and loud — no matter who it was — that I couldn't detect my own. My ability to know what other people needed and wanted was so much more developed than my ability to discern my own needs and wants, that in the presence of another person I had no idea how I felt.

So my time by myself was really precious. I wrote in my diary and read books and thought about the world. Alone, I could have "me" — and I couldn't when I was with other people, even the kindest and nicest of other people. I didn't love being alone. I felt lonely and like an outsider. But being alone felt necessary to being able to "have" myself. My parents and siblings, although they loved me, didn't seem very interested in me as a person in my own right. If I hadn't spent time alone, I would never have known that I even had my own thoughts and feelings about things.

The first time I ever had access to myself in the presence of another person was when I was 22 years old and I was being listened to by one of Gene Gendlin's students in the Changes community in Chicago.

This person wasn't impatiently waiting until I finished talking in order to give their own opinion. They were simply listening. Saying back what I said. Leaving space for me to sense and say more.

On that day I began to know that we can be ourselves in the presence of other people. And I got completely hooked on Focusing/listening partnership! Because what I learned was that "being myself" is not something static. In the presence of a person who is giving me space to explore how I feel, how I feel evolves. My inner sense takes forward steps of change. I grow. In evolving and growing, I become more myself. Amazing but true!

In the last chapter, I talked to you about allowing yourself to be moved by the requests of other people. How your confidence that you could say *yes* or *no* can allow you to soften in your boundaries without feeling like you are giving up something essential to yourself.

In this chapter, I want to share that the more grounded you feel in yourself, the more you're able to be impacted and influenced by other people and yet still be fully yourself. That who it is to be "myself" includes other people, as well as all that I have experienced.

There's a poem by Tennyson that includes the line:

I am a part of all that I have met

And he goes on to say that what we haven't yet experienced keeps on inviting us forward.

Yet all experience is an arch wherethro'
Gleams that untravell'd world whose margin fades
For ever and forever when I move.

Being alive means being ever-changing and at the same time, you can feel yourself as a person, as a presence, within that ever-changingness.

Let's try that as an exercise.

Take your time to bring awareness to your body... your whole body, here and now. Feeling the support under you, the contact of your feet on the ground, and the other places where your body is in contact with what you are sitting on. Resting into that support.

Take some time to get the feel of simply being present as yourself.

Exploring the feel of being you, being here right now.

"Being you" has a flavor, a quality... and that changes from time to time. So what you can feel now is the feel of being you right now.

Now, in your imagination, invite another person to join you. Someone you'd be glad to see right now. Let them sit down with you... feel your connection with them... and notice how your sense of yourself is impacted by the presence of that other person.

Has your sense of yourself changed? Do you still have your sense of yourself?

If it's hard to feel yourself in the presence of that other person, experiment with moving them farther away. Perhaps you could put a circle of light around them, as in the Figure Eight exercise. What does it take so that you can feel yourself in the presence of the other person?

Once you can feel yourself, try moving the other person closer again. Play with the boundary. That's right, this too is a boundary. How close can you get to that other person and still feel yourself?

Your practice today is to notice how easy or hard it is to feel in contact with yourself in the presence of other people, versus when you are alone. Notice how other people impact or influence your sense of being yourself. Notice if it is OK to experience "yourself" as something evolving and growing and changing.

Remember: It is OK to be who you are, even in the presence of other people.

DAY 21

Clear Communicating that Takes the Other into Account

A full, clear communication about boundaries
takes the other into account.
Let's find out how.

T oday I want to get very practical and spend some time with
how to actually tell other people about your boundaries.

Remember there are some essential preliminaries to communicating
with others about your boundaries.

1. **Being present to your feelings**. The most important
   boundary of all is your ability to be present to your own
   emotional states without being merged with them. We call
   this being Self-in-Presence.

2. **Being in touch with your own needs**. You have a right to
   your needs. You may not always get your needs met! But you
   have a right to have them and to honor them.

3. **Knowing you are worthwhile**. You have as much value as
   a human being with feelings and needs as anyone else. If
   there are parts of you that doubt or question this, they're
   connected to trauma and need your healing company. But
   those parts don't know the truth. The truth is, you have
   worth, as much worth as anyone.

You can feel, can't you, how these three fundamental abilities — all
of which can be developed within ourselves — are basic to being able
to communicate clearly about our boundaries with other people.

You've also seen that boundary questions bring up unhealed hurts
from the past that you still carry in your body. Those unhealed hurts
can lead you to fear abandonment if you're clear about your needs, to
keep silent if you fear the other person's anger, and to label yourself
with words like "selfish" if you don't put the other person first. They
can also cause you to hold yourself back from others, to put up walls,
to feel confused in interactions, and so on.

You learned a process for giving healing presence to the hurt "younger self" from the past — which, over time, can result in those old hurts having less power to hold you back in your present life.

You learned that when you feel confident about your right to set a clear boundary with another person, you can also feel more able to be moved and swayed by that person without losing a sense of your own ground. Being moved by another person is something you choose, not something you're helpless over.

So what happens, knowing all of this, when you now approach a situation where you need to communicate a boundary to another person?

Here's what I hope will happen:

- You'll be relaxed, curious, and open.

- You'll say what you need to say and you don't know how the person will react. You can't assume.

- You'll do your best to communicate clearly, and be interested in how that communication lands with the other person.

If they have a reaction, you might feel right about giving them some empathy for that, before coming back to restating your own boundary.

You might shift what you're asking because of what you heard from them, and you might not.

It's a flexible, dynamic, interactive situation. What I've found is that the more time I've spent giving healing presence to the hurt parts of me from the past, the more I am able to be fully here in the present with what is happening now: in touch with myself *and* able to hear the other person, even when the other person doesn't enjoy the boundary I set.

That might sound like this: "Mom, I'm no longer going to be able to visit you here every day. I love you and I care about how you are, and I will be here every other day or every third day at the very least."

Mom says something back. You respond, "Yes, I really hear that you are scared that something bad will happen to you here if I don't visit every day. Is that right?"

Mom says something more.

You say, "OK, I'm checking with myself, and I would be willing to call you on the days that I don't visit, to make sure something bad isn't happening. But that's the best I can do. And we can talk about this again next week after we try it."

Every situation is different, of course. So let's do an exercise where you try this process out with someone in your life, and a boundary you'd like to be able to set with this person.

Let's start by having you think of someone. Intimate relationship, friend, family member, co-worker, neighbor, someone in your community... Someone who has asked you to do something that you need to say *no* to; or someone you've been doing something for and you need to stop doing it; or someone you'd like to have do something for you; or someone who has been doing something that you feel violates your boundary and you need them to stop; or whatever comes to mind for you.

You can take a past situation in which you've already communicated, perhaps not in a way you are happy with, and do it over. Or a current situation you've not communicated in yet.

Let's pause to let you get that – the person and the boundary you want to set – before we go on.

Remember: if at any time in the process you don't feel relaxed, curious, and open, you can pause and turn to the part of you that got triggered, and give it some empathy and healing presence. That's what's so nice about practicing in our imagination!

So, imagine you're inviting this person into a conversation. And they say yes, we can talk.

First, remind them of the situation you're talking about, using descriptive language that they would agree with. Quoting words is a safe way to do this. For example:

> "Remember when you asked me to XYZ? I wanted to talk to you about that."

> "Remember when you asked me to organize your wedding dinner even though you aren't inviting me to be there? I wanted to talk to you about that."

> "Remember when we talked about keeping the kitchen table clear of your stuff?"

Next, state what you will or will not do, or what you want them to do or not do. See if you can do that without explaining.

"I will not be able to do that."

"I need to ask you to clear your stuff off the kitchen table before dinner tonight."

Now, find out how that lands with them.

"I wonder how that is for you to hear that?"

In your imagination, let the person respond. It's OK if they're not happy. Just let them respond as they probably would.

Now give empathy for the feelings you are hearing or guessing about in their response.

"I really hear that you're feeling hurt."

"I really hear that you don't feel you have time."

Take a moment to sense if you feel genuinely moved by what they said to want to adjust your boundary. If not, it's OK. If yes, let them know.

"OK, I am willing to make half of the calls, if you make the other half."

"OK, I am willing to clear off the table myself if you don't mind where I put your stuff."

And now, whether or not you were moved and made an adjustment, restate your boundary clearly.

"What I am saying is this."

Pause and take in what it was like to practice that kind of communication in your imagination. Obviously we don't know what would happen in a "real" situation. But that's part of the point of being relaxed, curious, and open. You don't know in advance what will happen, and you're ready to flexibly respond to what occurs in the moment. You're ready to stay in touch with yourself whatever occurs.

And if it doesn't seem easy, at least it's something to move toward!

Your practice today is to be relaxed, curious, and open in the situations that you meet today, whether they involve boundaries or not.

Remember: When you need to communicate about a boundary, be relaxed, curious and open... and if you can't be, give yourself some empathy first!

You have a right to your needs. You may not always get your needs met, but you have a right to have and honor them.

You have as much value as a human being with feelings and needs as anyone else.

The truth is, you have worth, as much worth as anyone.

Where do we go from here?

W ell done! If you've spent at least one day with every practice in this book, you're well on your way to healthier boundaries–and a healthier life!

As we've seen, working with issues around setting boundaries can bring up other issues and can get you in contact with a "younger you" who is carrying hurts from the past. This is a great result, because that "younger you" can heal, and life can feel much freer and easier than it has.

My recommended way to continue working with emotional issues is the Inner Relationship Focusing process. You can learn more about Focusing by visiting this special page of helpful resources we created just for you: https://focusingresources.com/hbmore

You might find it helpful to begin with my free e-course, Get Bigger Than What's Bugging You or my Learning Focusing audio set. Both of them will continue to provide you with support as you move forward. And if you found this helpful but want a little more support, there's also a video version of this content that includes access to me plus an online community of people working toward setting healthier boundaries.

Do keep in touch! I'd love to hear from you. You can reach me at ann@focusingresources.com. I'm proud of you and all I can say is: "You're doing great, keep going!"

About the Author

Ann Weiser Cornell was getting her PhD in Linguistics at the University of Chicago when she met and studied with Eugene Gendlin, the originator of Focusing, starting in 1972. Learning Focusing with him has led to a lifelong process of discovery and personal development.

In 1980, Eugene Gendlin invited Ann to assist with his Focusing workshops. This started her on a path to become a Focusing teacher, and in 1991, Ann joined with Barbara McGavin to create Inner Relationship Focusing, internationally recognized as one of the leading innovations in Focusing.

Ann has taught Inner Relationship Focusing in twenty countries, and her Focusing books and manuals have been translated into eleven other languages (Czech, Dari, Dutch, French, German, Hebrew, Italian, Japanese, Korean, Polish, and Spanish).

Ann is well-known in the Focusing world for her attention to the language that facilitates Focusing, her popular manuals, and her co-creation with Barbara McGavin of their Untangling® method. Untangling® applies Focusing to difficult areas such as addiction, depression, action blocks, self-criticism, and unfulfilled desire.

She is the author of five books on Focusing: her bestseller *The Power of Focusing* (1996), *The Radical Acceptance of Everything* (2005), *Focusing in Clinical Practice: The Essence of Change* (2013), *Presence: A Guide to Transforming Your Most Challenging Emotions* (2015), and *21 Days to Better Boundaries* (2020). Ann is authorized by the Focusing Institute in New York to offer the Institute's certification as Focusing Trainer.

On a personal note: Ann lives in Berkeley, California, with her life partner, Joseph McBride, noted film historian.

Also by
Ann Weiser Cornell

The Power of Focusing: A Practical Guide to Emotional Self-Healing

The Radical Acceptance of Everything: Living A Focusing Life

Focusing in Clinical Practice: The Essence of Change

Presence: A Guide to Transforming Your Most Challenging Emotions

Reviews on Amazon or Goodreads are not only appreciated, but they help other readers, like yourself, to find books that help shape their lives. Will you take a moment to leave the author a kind review, or to share on your social media how this book has impacted you? The author kindly thanks you.

Join the
Conversation

Ann Weiser Cornell founded Focusing Resources in 1985 as a way to support people who want to learn Inner Relationship Focusing. Today, Focusing Resources includes a worldwide community of thousands of people learning and teaching Focusing. Learn this powerful, research-based practice you can do on your own and get back in touch with the emotional wisdom of your body.

Join in on the conversation!

f facebook.com/focusingresources/

📷 instagram.com/focusingresources

▶ youtube.com/c/focusingresources

Made in the USA
Monee, IL
02 December 2022

19361075R00079